3 4028 07644 0735

HARRIS COUNTY PUBLIC LIBRARY

J 970.4 Wad
Wade, Mary Dodson
Texas native peoples

$33.50
ocn231948392
Rev. and update 06/02/2011

WITHDRAWN

D0772757

Revised and Updated

Texas
Native Peoples

Mary Dodson Wade

Heinemann Library
Chicago, Illinois

© 2004, 2008 Heinemann Library
a division of Reed Elsevier Inc.
Chicago, Illinois

Customer Service 888-454-2279

Visit our website at **www.heinemannlibrary.com**

All rights reserved. No part of this publication may be reproduced or transmitted in any form or by any means, electronic or mechanical, including photocopying, recording, taping, or any information storage and retrieval system, without permission in writing from the publisher.

Designed by Kimberly R. Miracle and Betsy Wernert
Photo Research by Tracy Cummins
Printed and bound in China by Leo Paper Group Ltd

12 11 10 09 08
10 9 8 7 6 5 4 3 2 1

New edition ISBNs: 978-1-4329-1152-2 (hardcover)
                   978-1-4329-1159-1 (paperback)

The Library of Congress has cataloged the first edition as follows:
Wade, Mary Dodson.
  Texas Native peoples / Mary Dodson Wade.
     v. cm. -- (Heinemann state studies)
Includes bibliographical references and index.
Contents: Early people -- Native Texans in historic times -- Sweeping changes from the north -- Peaceful neighbors from the east -- Texas Native peoples today.
  ISBN 1-4034-0688-X -- ISBN 1-4034-2697-X
  1. Indians of North America--Texas--History--
Juvenile literature. 2. Indians of North America--Texas--
Social life and customs--Juvenile
literature. [1. Indians of North America--Texas.]
I. Title. II. Series.
  E78.T4W25 2003
  976.4004'97--dc21
                   2003009560

Acknowledgments
The author and publishers are grateful to the following for permission to reproduce copyright material:

Cover photograph reproduced with permission of ©National Archives Washington DC

p. 5 Warren Morgan/Corbis; **p. 6** Communications Branch/Texas Parks and Wildlife Department; **p. 7** Courtesty of Interpretations and Exhibits Branch/Texas Parks and Wildlife Department; **p. 8T** Carter Sisney Photography; **p. 8B** Jim Zintgraff/The Rock Art Foundation; **p. 9** The Mariners' Museum/Corbis; **p. 10** Tim Thompson/Corbis; **p. 13** Werner Forman/Corbis; **p. 14** The Gilcrease Museum; **p. 16** D. Robert & Lorri Franz/Corbis; **pp. 20T, 26, 31** Smithsonian American Art Museum, Washington, DC/Art Resource, NY; **pp. 20B, 24, 30** Lawrence T. Jones III Collection, Austin, Texas; **pp. 22, 25** Bettmann/Corbis; **p. 27** Manuscript Acee Blue Eagle Papers: Paintings and Prints by Indian Artists: Mopope, Stephen, Smithsonian Institution National Anthropological Archives; **pp. 28, 40** Corbis; **p. 29** Western History Collections/University of Oklahoma Libraries; **p. 33** Dennis Cook/AP Photo; **p. 35** Peter Turnley/Corbis; **p. 33T** North Wind Picture Archives; **p. 36** University of Texas Institute of Texan Cultures at San Antonio; **pp. 39, 42** Library of Congress; **p. 41** Marilyn "Angel" Wynn/Nativestock; **p. 43** Greg Leitich Smith

Every effort has been made to contact copyright holders of any material reproduced in this book. Any omissions will be rectified in subsequent printings if notice is given to the publisher.

Disclaimer
All the Internet addresses (URLs) given in this book were valid at the time of going to press. However, due to the dynamic nature of the Internet, some addresses may have changed, or sites may have changed or ceased to exist since publication. While the author and publisher regret any inconvenience this may cause readers, no responsibility for any such changes can be accepted by either the author or the publisher.

Contents

Some words are shown in bold, **like this**. You can find out what they mean by looking in the glossary.

Texas's Earliest People

The first people to enter North America came during the last **Ice Age**. At that time, **glaciers** covered much of North America. A land bridge stretching across the Bering Sea connected Asia with Alaska. Most scientists believe that people began to **migrate** across this land bridge from Asia into North America about 40,000 years ago.

Groups of these people eventually reached what is now Texas about 11,200 years ago. What is known about these people comes from **artifacts**, or the things they left behind. Scientists study these people's bones, and their tools, pottery, and baskets, as well as the bones of the animals they ate. They also study the pictures that these people drew on rocks.

Migration Routes

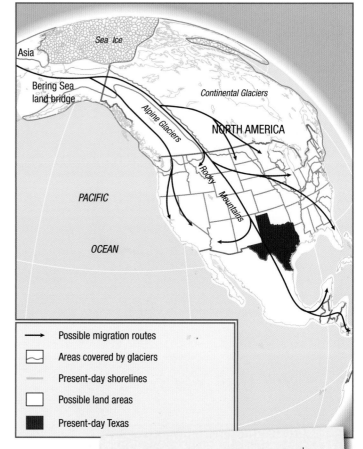

- → Possible migration routes
- ∿ Areas covered by glaciers
- — Present-day shorelines
- ☐ Possible land areas
- ■ Present-day Texas

Most American Indians believe their people have always been in the Americas. But most scientists think that Paleo-Indians, the **ancestors** of historic Indians, probably came from Asia, across the Bering Sea land bridge.

Texas's Native Peoples

Paleo-Indians	Archaic	Late Prehistoric	Historic
9200 BCE to 6000 BCE	6000 BCE to 500 CE	500 CE to 1500 CE	1500 CE to Present

Paleo-Indians, 9200 to 6000 BCE

During the last Ice Age, the **climate** in Texas was cool. Paleo-Indians hunted giant mammoths, mastodons, and bison. Scientists have found spear points dating back about 11,000 years, which the Paleo-Indians used to hunt these animals. About a thousand years later, the huge animals the Paleo-Indians hunted began to die out. Scientists have found spear points with the bones of ancient bison that are now **extinct**.

Evidence shows that Paleo-Indians lived in east Texas, but no mammoths or bison roamed there. In west Texas, the skull of a woman at least 8,000 years old was found on a ranch near Midland. The richest area for artifacts is the Lower Pecos River. People lived in the canyons near the Rio Grande about 10,500 years ago.

Archaic Period, 6000 BCE to 500 CE

During the Archaic period, plants and animals that we know today developed. The Indians of the Archaic period used many stone tools to hunt game animals such as bison and deer.

Archaic people also gathered berries and nuts and dug up roots for food. In central Texas, there are rock mounds where people cooked plants. Along Texas's coast and along inland rivers, Archaic people left mounds of shells from the **mollusks** they ate.

Spear points were made in a process called knapping. The knapper first used a stone to chip a general shape. Then softer blows with a deer antler made the final shape. Finally, a small stone pressed against the edge made it sharp.

What Were Spear Points Made Of?

Many of the spear points that Paleo-Indians and Archaic Indians used were made of flint. Flint is a very hard stone that makes good spear points. It flakes off when struck by a hard object. Alibates flint is found only in a 10-square-mile (26-square-kilometer) area north of Amarillo. Early people traded the maroon and white flint long distances. Alibates flint is named for Allie Bates, the cowboy who found it.

Over the centuries, the climate in south Texas became hotter and drier, so the bison left. Desert plants started to grow, and people adapted to the warm climate. Archaic Indians wore little clothing. For cooler weather, they wore robes made of rabbit skins. They wove plant stalks together for sandals.

During the Archaic period, Indians often lived in rock shelters. Overhanging rocks formed shelters when layers of limestone rock crumbled away along the banks of the Rio Grande and its **tributaries** in south Texas. About 25 to 30 people lived in a rock shelter. Sleeping pits with grass and woven mats lined the back wall. Cooking pits were near the front of the shelter.

Archaic people in south Texas hunted or gathered rabbits, deer, fish, rodents, birds, reptiles, freshwater clams, and land snails. Women caught grasshoppers and placed them in pouches made from cactus pads. About 75 percent of what the people ate came from plants.

The Fate Bell Rock Shelter is located at Seminole Canyon State Park and Historic Site, about 30 miles (48 kilometers) west of Comstock. Indians lived there from about 7000 BCE to 1500 CE.

Archaic hunters used a curved stick that looked like a boomerang to hunt rabbits. They often hunted in small groups in order to first trap the animals.

Mosquito Repellent

Along the coast, mosquitoes are a big problem. Several prehistoric groups smeared themselves with alligator grease to keep off the pesky insects.

Women used digging sticks to collect plant bulbs, which they baked in pits heated with rocks. Women also ground mesquite beans, seeds, dried berries, walnuts, pecans, and acorns. They used a *mano*, which means "hand" in Spanish, to crush them against a large, flat stone called a *metate*. Acorns were not good to eat until they had been soaked in water. Ground food was mixed with water and made into cakes or mush.

Indians during the Archaic period roasted meat over a fire. They ate fruits, flowers, and berries raw or sun-dried. They also ate the fruit of the prickly pear cactus raw. Their cooking pot was a piece of animal hide tied loosely to a tripod made of three sticks. Water was poured into the hide and heated by adding hot rocks.

Atlatl

Archaic hunters often used a tool called an atlatl to hunt large animals. *Atlatl* (AT-lat-uhl) is an Aztec word for "spear thrower." The Aztec were a group of Indians who lived in Mexico. The 18-inch (46-centimeter) throwing stick increased the speed and force of the spear. A hook held the end of the spear.

Rock drawings of **shamans** have been found several places around Texas. This one is from Panther Cave in the Lower Pecos area of south Texas.

Rock art began to appear in the area that is now Texas during the Archaic period. The Lower Pecos area in south Texas has some of the finest rock art in North America. Some painted areas are 30 feet (9 meters) long and 12 feet (4 meters) high. Pictures were finger-painted, spatter painted, or marked like crayons. Other artists used brushes made from the leaves of desert plants.

Some of the oldest rock art in the Americas is found in south Texas, west of Del Rio. Seminole Canyon State Historical Park has pictographs that are 4,000 to 6,000 years old. They show animals, people, graceful stick figures, and geometric designs.

Late Prehistoric Times, 500 to 1500 CE

Corn, also called maize, developed in the Americas. People began to farm corn in late prehistoric times. This allowed them to settle in towns, since they did not have to follow animals for food as much. Corn, beans, and squash were important crops in prehistoric America.

Indian groups during the Late Prehistoric period began to name themselves. Usually, they simply called themselves "the people." These groups developed into the American Indian tribes of historic times. The names by which we know these people were given to them by others.

Shamans

Shamans were important people in many Indian groups, even as far back as the Archaic period. These people were the center of the hunter-gatherer society. They conducted birth and death **ceremonies** and cured illness. They explained natural objects like stars and told stories. Indians believed that shamans spoke to spirits and took animal shapes.

Indians of prehistoric and historic times usually roasted meat over a fire, like this. Leftovers would be dried and saved for later.

Early Caddo

The Caddo were a **confederation** of several American Indian groups. They came to the Neches (NAY-chez) River valley in northeast Texas around 700 CE. Like other American Indian groups who lived around the Mississippi River valley, the early Caddo were mound builders. They built wooden temples on top of those flat mounds. People carried dirt in large baskets to build these mounds in stages. Some of the mounds at Caddo Mounds State Historic Site near Alto have been **excavated** and provide a lot of information about how the early Caddo lived.

Caddo houses were about 25 to 45 feet (8 to 14 meters) across and looked like tall beehives. The supporting poles were covered with **thatch** tied with grape vines. About 30 people lived in a house.

The Caddo were tall. They decorated their bodies with tattoos. The early Caddo were peaceful farmers. Men fished and used bows and arrows to hunt bear, deer, small animals, and birds. The Caddo gathered hickory nuts, grapes, and other fruit. They also raised beans, pumpkins, and squash. The Caddo stored extra crops for times of **drought**. The Caddo used clay to make fine bowls, jars, and long-stemmed smoking pipes. They created small human and animal figurines that may have been toys. They wove cane baskets and made unusual black leather clothing from the skins of young deer.

In early Caddo society, a ruling class and priests lived near the temples and controlled the government and religion. Workers lived in scattered houses near fields. The Caddo exchanged goods with people in central Texas. They also traded with people as far away as present-day Illinois.

Texas's First Tribes

The first written records about American Indians began in the 1500s, at the time of the arrival of European explorers and settlers. The first records included tribes along the coast, where the explorers landed. These records included descriptions of the Indian tribes in Texas.

Texas's First Native Tribes

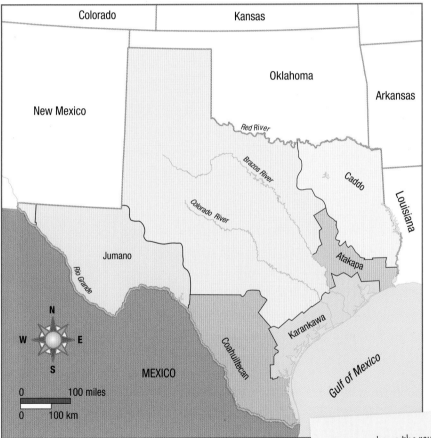

This map shows the rough location of the first tribes of Texas. The tribes did move around to hunt and trade however. They did not really recognize strict borders.

Late Caddo

When Spanish explorers entered east Texas in 1542, three major Caddo groups lived in the area. The Natchitoches (NAK-uh-tish) lived in northwestern Louisiana. The Kadohadacho (kad-oh-hah-DAH-choh) were in northeast Texas near the bend of the Red River. The name *Caddo* comes from them. The Hasinai (hah-see-NEYE) lived near Caddo Mounds farther south.

Tejas

The Hasinai greeted the Spaniards with a word that the Spaniards understood to be *Tejas* (TAY-hahs). The Spaniards thought it was the Hasinai's name, and they established Mission San Francisco de los Tejas near Caddo Mounds. Actually, the word *Tejas* is a greeting that means "friend." Texas gets its name from *Tejas*.

After the United States bought the Louisiana Territory from the French in 1803, the Caddo moved west to get away from incoming settlers. In 1859 the United States government moved them to Indian Territory in present-day Oklahoma.

Atakapa

The Atakapa (uh-TAK-uh-puh) lived in the coastal swamps of southeast Texas. Much of what is known about the Atakapa comes from the descriptions written by Europeans. According to these descriptions, the Atakapa were short and heavyset with dark skin. They went barefoot, even in winter. Men wore **breechcloths**, but in winter added a bison robe with the tail attached. The underside of the robe was painted red with black designs. Women cut a hole in the hides and slipped them over their heads.

Atakapa houses were made of poles covered with vines. Their pottery came from other tribes with whom they traded. They used dugout boats to travel to nearby islands. The Atakapa people were organized into small bands. Each band had a leader called a headman. There was no main chief. When groups met each other, they made loud wailing noises. The greeting was the same for both good and bad news.

Each band had a specific territory where they hunted deer and bear with bows and arrows. The Atakapa also speared fish. The spears had floats on them so that the owner could get the spear back. The Atakapa also ate shellfish and underwater roots. They gathered wild plants and bird eggs. Alligators provided meat, oil, and hides.

The Atakapa did not have temples. But the **shaman's** hut was sometimes placed on higher ground on a mound of shells. The shaman had a powder that he sprinkled on water to stun the fish and make them easy to catch.

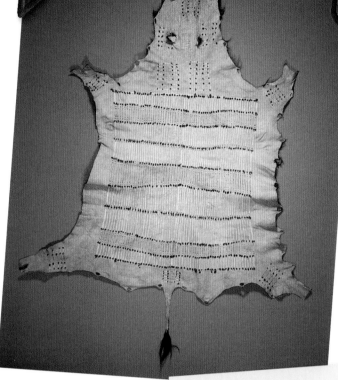

This is an example of the bison robes worn by Atakapa men during the winter. The tail is still attached, and the red and black designs are still visible.

French trade with the Atakapa led Spanish leaders to build **missions** in Texas in order to defend their territory. Contact with Europeans brought many diseases, which destroyed the Atakapa. American Indians had no resistance to European diseases. So, thousands of American Indians died from exposure to diseases such as **smallpox**. By 1908, only nine known Atakapa were living.

Atakapa Creation Story

The Atakapa creation story says that the Atakapa people came out of a giant oyster shell in the ocean. They believed that a supreme being had given them rules to follow. At death, those who did good deeds went above the earth. Those who did evil went under the earth.

Karankawa

The Karankawa (kuh-RAHN-kuh-wah) lived on the Texas coast from western Galveston Bay to Corpus Christi. Their name meant "dog lovers." The Karankawa raised and kept dogs that the Europeans thought looked like foxes.

Small bands of 30 or 40 Karankawa moved about looking for food. They ate fish, shellfish, and turtles. Hunters had red cedar bows that were almost as tall as they were. Karankawa men were tall and muscular. They wore breechcloths or nothing at all, painted and tattooed their bodies, and wore a piece of **cane** through the lower lip. They were powerful runners and expert swimmers, and they enjoyed contests. Wrestling was such a favorite that neighboring tribes called them "Wrestlers." Women painted and tattooed their bodies and wore skirts made of animal skin.

This is a drawing of a Karankawa man and woman. It gives an idea of the size of the bows hunters used and what their clothes looked like.

Karankawa houses were made of willow poles covered with skins or mats. The Karankawa also made dugout canoes big enough to carry a family and its goods. They waterproofed baskets and pottery with **asphalt** that washed ashore. Karankawa groups communicated with each other using smoke signals. The groups sometimes gathered together for dances.

The Karankawa's first contact with Europeans came when shipwrecked Spanish *conquistador* Cabeza de Vaca landed at Galveston in 1528. The Karankawa remained a hunter-fisher-gatherer society. They refused to stay at Spanish missions. Later, the Mexican government tried to keep them west of the Lavaca River, away from the white settlements, but they always returned. In the mid–1840s, the Karankawas moved into Mexico, then back to Rio Grande City. The Europeans in each place forced them to leave. By 1854, the Karankawa were all but wiped out.

Coahuiltecan

Farther down the coast from the Karankawas, Coahuiltecan (Ko-uh-WEEL-tee-kan) groups hunted and fished from Corpus Christi to Mexico. Their name came from the language they spoke.

Some Coahuiltecan men plucked their hair back from the forehead. Tattooed lines ran from the nose up to the hair. Other tattooed lines decorated the face and body. The men sometimes wore breechcloths decorated with seeds and animal teeth. They went barefoot, but wore sandals when walking on thorny ground.

The Coahuiltecan ate deer, rabbits, rats, birds, and snakes, but food was scarce. They hunted deer, antelope, and javelina (hah-vuh-LEE-nuh), a piglike animal, with bows and arrows. They used a curved club as both a digging stick and weapon. Men ran long distances and could tire out a deer. On the coast, they forced animals into the water where they would drown or could be shot with arrows. When a hunter killed a deer, he marked a trail. Women then brought in the animal. The hunter received the hide, but the meat was given to others.

Coahuiltecans roasted bulbs from the maguey plants and gathered mesquite beans. They ate prickly pear cactus flowers and fruit and squeezed water from cactus pads. The women carried water in pouches made from the pads. They could carry 12 to 14 of these in a woven netting with a **tumpline**.

The State of Coahuila

The northern Mexican state of Coahuila was named after the Coahuiltecans. Before independence, Texas was joined with Coahuila as a state in Mexico.

Coahuiltecan bands resisted coming to Spanish missions. By the mid–1800s, they had disappeared. Some may have escaped to Mexico. Disease and hostile Apache and Comanche warriors killed many others.

The Coahuiltecan used pit traps to catch javelinas. They made pits about 5 feet (1.5 meters) wide and 8 feet (2.4 meters) deep and covered them with leaves and twigs to hide them.

Jumano

The Jumano (hoo-MAHN-oh) are a mystery. They appear in Spanish records around 1500–1700 CE, then disappear. Nothing remains of their language to tell where they came from or where they went.

Two Jumano groups in Texas were widely separated. One group farmed on the Rio Grande south of El Paso. They also went on hunting trips. These Jumano lived in **tepees** while hunting, but had **adobe** houses along the Rio Grande. The other Jumano group lived along the Red River. They may actually have been the same group, because the Jumano moved across the state on trading trips.

The horizontal stripes on their faces made the Jumano easy to recognize as they approached their trading partners. The Jumano carried corn, dried squashes, and beans from the farming areas. They traded these foods as well as mesquite beans, cloth, **turquoise**, unusual feathers, pigments, shells, and salt for hides, meat, and other bison products. Through trade, they also supplied Spanish goods and horses to other tribes.

In the 1700s, the Apache advanced south and cut off Jumano trade routes. Eventually, the Jumano had no land of their own. Some may have joined the Apache. However, the Jumano disappeared long before white settlers arrived.

Native Tribes Today

None of the groups living in Texas when Europeans arrived has a **reservation** in the state today. Many individuals died as the result of diseases brought by the Europeans. Only the Caddo in Oklahoma remain as a distinct tribe.

Tribes of the Plains Culture

The pressure of advancing settlers eventually pushed new American Indian groups into Texas. The biggest change for these Indians in Texas and across the Great Plains came when the Spanish brought horses to North America. Until that time, Indians walked and used dogs to carry their possessions. After Plains Indians learned to ride horses, they moved freely across the Great Plains, and the Plains **culture**, which relied on the bison, developed.

Texas Plains Tribes

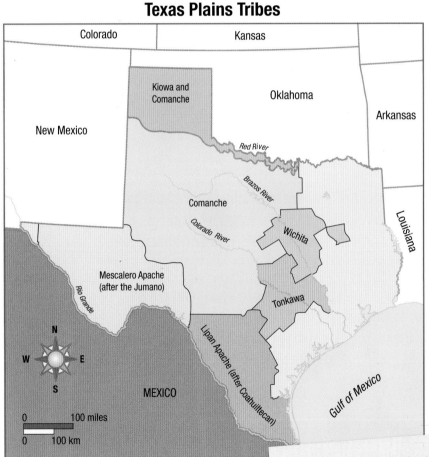

This map shows the rough location of the Plains Indians in Texas. The Mescalero Apache quickly moved on to New Mexico. The Kiowa Apache lived with the Kiowa.

Millions of bison roamed the Great Plains. Bison supplied everything the Plains Indians needed. Bison meat was eaten raw, cooked, or dried. Hooves provided glue to make arrows. **Sinew** was used for thread and bowstrings. Bison hair was braided into ropes and belts. Horns were made into cups and spoons. Bones were shaped into tools. Hides provided covering for moveable houses, such as **tepees**. Clothing, robes, shields, and bags all came from bison. Even bison brains were smeared on hides to soften them.

When the bison were almost completely killed off by United States hunters, so was the livelihood of the tribes of the Great Plains. The United States created **reservations** for the tribes in Indian Territory, in present-day Oklahoma. Many Texas tribes were forced out of the state in 1839, by order of Texas President Mirabeau Lamar. Their final removal occurred in 1859.

Wichita

One of the first Europeans to meet the Wichita was the Spanish explorer Francisco Vásquez de Coronado. He explored the area around southern Kansas in 1542. The Wichita were actually made up of four loosely associated groups, which were the Wichita, Waco, Tawakoni (Tah-WAH-kohn-ee) or Kichai, and Taovaya (tah-oh-VAH-yah). The Osage, a group hostile to the Wichita, pushed the Wichita south. The Wichita then settled on the Red River at Spanish Fort. The Waco group advanced down to central Texas, near what is today the city of Waco. In the early 1800s, Wichita were trading goods from the Great Plains to Louisiana.

The Wichita had darker skin than most tribes. The men painted circles around their eyes and called themselves "raccoon eyes." Both men and women tattooed lines and geometric shapes on their faces. Wichita warriors painted their brave deeds on their robes or tepees.

Wichita villages were located along rivers and had 100 or more neatly arranged houses. Open shelters next to the houses provided a place to work, rest, and store extra food. The Wichita were excellent farmers. They grew corn, melons, beans, and pumpkins. After the Wichita began using horses, the men hunted bison during the winter. They lived in tepees while on the hunt.

Wichita marriages involved the groom giving horses to the bride's father or brother. The groom's parents provided a feast for the bride's family. The new couple lived with the bride's family.

Wichita women tattooed their faces and wore dresses made of tanned hides that went down to their ankles. They sometimes used elk teeth to decorate clothing and make jewelry.

The cone-shaped houses of the Wichita were 15 to 30 feet (4.6 to 9 meters) across and made of poles covered with grass. Beds stood off the floor on poles.

When a person died, he or she was buried in a shallow grave with things they would need in the afterlife. Men were buried with tools, and women were buried with domestic items, such as cooking tools. Mourning family and friends cut their hair and gave away some of their own possessions. After four days, friends prepared a feast for the family.

Jerky and Pemmican

Jerky and pemmican were popular foods among American Indians. Jerky was meat roasted over a low fire and cut into strips. Pemmican was pounded meat, nuts, and berries stuffed into animal intestines. Both were nutritious and easy to store for later use.

The Wichita respected a **deity** called Man-Never-Known-On-Earth. In their creation story, this god made a land that floated on water. He gave a man and a woman an ear of corn and bows and arrows. This first man became Morning Star, and the woman was the moon goddess Bright Morning Star.

By the mid–1800s, the Wichita lived in the Wichita Mountains of Oklahoma. After the Civil War in 1865, they were placed on a **reservation** with the Waco and Tawakoni groups.

Tonkawa

Tonkawa (TAHNG-kuh-wah) is a Waco word meaning "they stay all together." The Tonkawa were loosely connected bands that united by the 1800s. They lived on the Edwards Plateau, near present-day Austin, and had a tribal chief.

The Tonkawa hunted and gathered fruits, herbs, berries, acorns, and pecans. They traded pecans to settlers. After the Comanche, another Indian group, cut them off from the lands where bison roamed, the Tonkawa ate deer, rabbits, skunks, rats, and tortoises. Rattlesnake was a **delicacy**. The Tonkawa avoided wolves, probably for religious reasons. The sacred Wolf Dance was performed in secret.

Tonkawa houses were low tepees made with bison hides. When they could no longer get hides, they made brush houses. Tribal members belonged to the **clans** of their mothers. Tonkawa men wore a very long **breechcloth** and leggings. In cooler weather they put on hide shirts and robes. Women wore deerskin skirts and tattooed their upper bodies.

Tonkawa **shamans** treated the sick. As death approached, they circled the dying person and put their hands on him or her. A second circle stood behind and touched the shoulders of the people in the first circle. After death, the person's hair was cut, the face painted yellow, and the body wrapped in a skin robe. Friends brought gifts to be buried with the body.

This is an 1898 photograph of Sentele, or Grant Richards, a Tonkawa chief. Tonkawa men had long hair they parted in the middle and wore loose or braided. They wore bone or shell beads and earrings and put feathers in their hair.

After three days of mourning, relatives and friends brought food, clothing, and household furnishings to replace those buried at the funeral. Tonkawa buried the dead with their heads to the west, so that the spirit of the dead could go in that direction. People slept with their feet to the west so that they would not be taken to the underworld too early.

Tonkawa thought that mistletoe was poison. They rubbed mistletoe juice on their arrows and later on the ends of their guns. Warriors also used lances. They carried shields made out of bison hides and used padded jackets for protection. The Tonkawa were warlike but friendly with white settlers. Later, they acted as scouts for the United States army while fighting other Indian groups. This caused other tribes to attack the Tonkawa when they were sent to Indian Territory.

Apache

Three groups of Apache lived in Texas. The Lipan (lee-PAHN) are the most well known Apache tribe that lived in Texas. They lived in the Texas Hill Country by the 1700s. Mescalero (mes-kuh-LAR-oh) Apache lived in New Mexico by 1855. Kiowa Apache lived along the Red River and had more in common with the Kiowa Indians there.

Apache men wore breechcloths, leggings, and moccasins. In the winter they added a **buckskin** shirt and blanket. Women wore knee-length deerskin skirts, snug-fitting leggings, and high moccasins. Their shirts were also made of deerskin. Young girls wore dresses of beaded buckskin. The bottom of the dress was fringed with brass or tin ornaments.

In early days, the Apache had gardens in which they grew corn, beans, squash, and pumpkins. But Comanche raids in the 1700s forced the Apache to abandon their farms. The Apache hunted bison, deer, antelope, javelinas, rats, and wild turkeys. They traded meat, hides, **tallow**, and salt with American Indian groups in New Mexico. In return they received cotton blankets, pottery, corn, and small green stones that were probably **turquoise**. The Apache kept cattle for food and used the stomachs of cattle or bison to hold water. Women carried large baskets of water with the help of a **rawhide** strap.

Apache groups were small, usually several extended families banded together. A respected person was chosen as the leader. Marriages were arranged by families. The groom was obligated to take care of his wife's family. If the wife died, her sister was offered to the husband. A woman could not leave if her husband died. Often she married her husband's brother.

Tonkawa Names

To keep from angering the spirits of people who had died, Tonkawa names were never used more than once. Tonkawa borrowed Comanche and European names after they ran out of their own.

When a child was born, it was held up to the north, south, east, and west and shown to the Sun. The father named the child a few days after birth, usually for something in nature. Children were rarely punished, and grandparents taught them skills they needed to know.

Apache warriors earned respect by performing brave deeds. They were excellent horsemen and counted wealth by how many horses they owned. A warrior's favorite horse was staked outside his tepee at night. Even after they had guns, the Apache still preferred their 4-foot- (1.2 meter-) long mulberry bows. The Apache made bow strings out of split deer or bison **sinews** twisted together. Warriors also carried an oval bison-hide shield that turned away arrows and bullets unless hit straight on.

Apaches were afraid of spirits. Mourners walked home from the grave by different routes to confuse the spirits. Names of the dead were not spoken for fear the ghost would return and take the living to the underworld. Relatives did not eat during the time of mourning. The Apache believed that shamans could control or predict events. Near the end of life, shamans often transferred their power to younger shamans.

This is a rare 19th-century photograph of a Lipan Apache chief (center) who served as a scout for the U.S. army. It was taken sometime in the 1870s at Fort Clark, Texas.

The Lipan Apache were friendly toward white settlers in Texas. Gradually, however, the Apache were forced out by settlers and went to Mexico. For years they raided along the border between Texas and Mexico. Finally, in 1873, United States army Colonel Ranald S. Mackenzie led soldiers into Mexico and attacked Lipan villages. Lipan Apache survivors went to the Mescalero Apache **reservation** in New Mexico.

Apache tepees were large enough for a dozen people. Beds were made of grass or cedar twigs several inches deep, covered with hides, fur side up.

Kiowa and Kiowa Apache

The Kiowa and Kiowa Apache were latecomers to Texas. The two groups were the same in almost every practice except language. It is believed that the Kiowa once lived in western Montana. They were driven out of that region by other American Indian groups in 1780. Soon afterward, they were in Oklahoma's Wichita Mountains. The Kiowa and Kiowa Apache made a lasting peace with the Comanche in 1840.

The Kiowa were organized into bands. Every Kiowa group had a headman who directed hunts and decided where to camp. The leader was generous, because the band was free to leave him if they chose.

Bison, deer, and antelope were the Kiowa's main food, but they did not eat bear, birds, or fish. When hunting, mounted Kiowa men formed a circle around small **game** and forced the animals toward women and children, who then caught the animals by hand. There was no shooting unless the animals broke out of the circle. In large bison hunts, men surrounded the bison. They then shot the animals or forced them over a cliff. The Kiowa did not farm. They traded for plant food or took it from others. The Kiowa were often on the move and could break down their camp in 30 minutes. They carried nothing breakable. They used bison or cow stomachs to hold water.

Kiowa men let their hair grow as long as possible on the left side. It was cut on the right side to show off earrings. A scalp lock was left hanging down behind. Women parted their hair in the middle and wore it in two braids, or loose with a headband.

The Kiowa were described as tall and graceful. Kiowa clothing was made of **buckskin**. The Kiowa wore jewelry made from Mexican silver coins and decorated clothing and horses with metal ornaments. Kiowa war bonnets had feathers, horns, and a headband made of colored beads.

Kiowa tepees were made of tanned hides decorated with artistic paintings. Beds were made of light willow rods lying across several poles. These were covered with bison skins and blankets.

Kiowa boys married at age 16 and girls at age 14. The groom offered horses to the bride's parents. Once married, the couple usually lived with the bride's parents. Important men had several wives. Women did a huge amount of work, and having several wives made the work easier.

Kiowa children were named by a grandparent. Names came from important events or deeds of **ancestors**. Old men near death often gave their names to younger men and then went nameless the rest of their lives. Names of the dead were not used or even spoken. When people died, they were buried in high places that were not easy to get to. Their goods were buried with them. Mourning lasted several days.

Indian Sign Language

The Kiowa are said to have developed the sign language that all Plains Indians used and understood.

The Kiowa Five

The Kiowa were very artistic and continued that **tradition** in the 20th century. In the 1920s, under the leadership of their art teacher at the University of Oklahoma, a group of five Kiowa artists gained international attention for their paintings.

This silkscreen painting (below) was done by Stephen Mopope, one of the Kiowa Five. It shows two Indian dancers and a drummer, all wearing feathers.

The Kiowa worshiped the Sun as their main god, but they believed that all things had certain powers. Owls, for instance, contained the souls of the dead. The Kiowa believed heaven was across the western ocean. It was a joyous place where game was plentiful, and horses were large and swift.

The Kiowa usually held the Sun Dance in the middle of June. All the tribes came together for the ten-day event. Everything followed strict **rituals**. The head of a freshly killed bison was placed on the 20-foot- (6-meter-) tall medicine lodge pole. Tepees circled the lodge in a set order. The sacred Sun Dance image, the *Taime*, was set up on the west side. The dance itself lasted four days. Before everyone left, old clothes, and sometimes a horse, were tied to the lodge pole as sacrifices.

The Kiowa were finally forced onto an Oklahoma **reservation** in 1875. Less than 20 years later, their land was divided and sold. In order to survive, the Kiowa quickly learned to live in the white **culture**.

The Kiowa were unusual because they kept a calendar history on an animal hide. A series of pictures spiraled from the outside to the center of the hide. Markings showed winter and summer seasons with their important events. This Kiowa hide calendar is from around 1895.

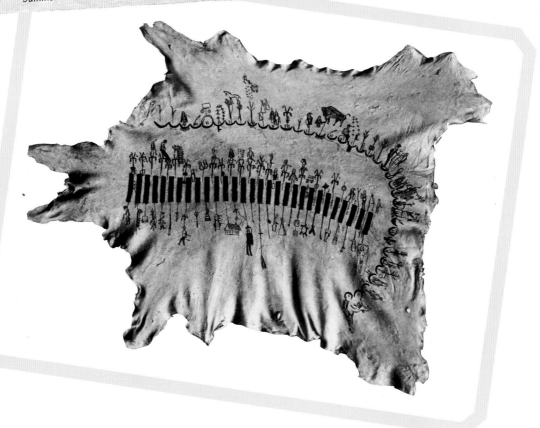

Comanche

The Comanche were some of the finest horsemen in the world. Comanche children often learned to ride a horse at a very young age. The horse was the center of the Comanche life and economy. Both men and women owned horses. The Comanche were the only tribe to breed horses. They also captured or stole them. They swept down out of the Colorado mountains and into Texas and became "lords of the Southern Plains."

Cynthia Ann and Quanah Parker

Cynthia Ann Parker was 11 years old when a group of Comanche and other Indians attacked and killed most of her family in Limestone County, Texas, in 1836. Cynthia Ann was taken to live with the Comanche. In 1847 she married Chief Peta Nocona and had two sons and a little girl. A group including some Texas Rangers attacked their camp in 1860. Cynthia Ann was taken to the Parker family, but she tried to return to the Comanche. She was never able to return, and she died sometime around 1870.

Cynthia Ann's teenage son Quanah (below) escaped the raid of 1860. He joined the Quahadi Comanche and rose to be their chief. After the Comanche went to the reservation, he learned the ways of white culture and became a strong voice for his people. He was a friend of Texas rancher Charles Goodnight and hunted with President Theodore Roosevelt on land that had once been his home.

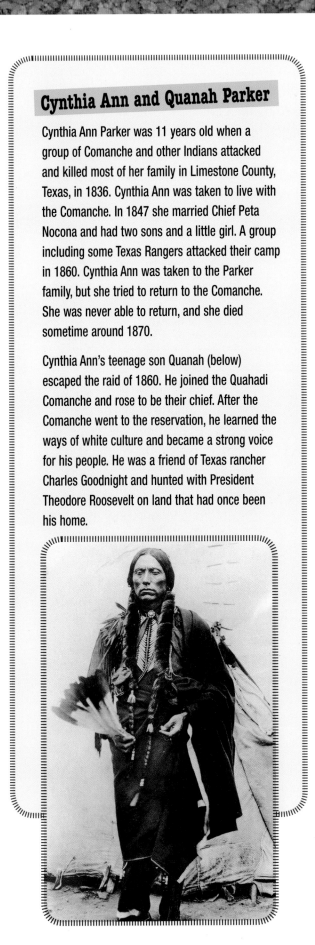

The Comanche were never a unified group. Different bands were named for food, and each had a general territory. The Penateka Comanche (Honey Eaters) lived west of the Cross Timbers between the place where the Colorado and Brazos Rivers start. The Kotsoteka (Buffalo Eaters) were the most warlike Comanche. The last Plains Indians to surrender to United States forces were the Quahadi (Antelope) Comanche, who lived in the Llano Estacado, in northwest Texas.

Comanche camps were set up along streams in no particular order. **Tepees** made out of hide were 12 to 14 feet (3.7 to 4.2 meters) high, but a chief's was larger. The door faced away from the wind. Beds were made of animal skins.

Comanche men wore braids and painted the part in their hair. They wore a yellow or black feather in a scalp lock. They plucked their eyebrows and beards and might have as many as ten ear piercings for shell or silver earrings. Their clothing included a **breechcloth**, leggings, and moccasins. Only important war chiefs had feather headdresses. Some chiefs wore bison horns.

Comanche women wore decorated **buckskin** shirts and skirts with uneven hemlines. Moccasins were decorated with beads, fringe, and little bits of iron called tinklers. Comanche women wore their hair short. They painted their faces with red and yellow lines above and below the eyes. They painted their ears red inside.

Newborn babies were wrapped in soft skins and strapped to a **cradleboard**. There was no set time to name a child. Children were called by pet names until they were officially named. At the naming **ceremony**, the **shaman** blew smoke in all four directions. Then he held the baby up to each of the four directions. Names were considered magical. A sickly baby would be given another name to get rid of the sickness.

This photograph of a Comanche woman and her baby was taken between 1905 and 1910. Comanche women often strapped their babies in cradleboards to their backs while they worked.

The Comanche never planted crops. They traded for food or took it. They hunted with bows made of hickory, a very hard wood. They used a 3-foot- (91-centimeter-) long bow that was easy to handle on horseback. The bow was strung with split bison or deer **sinew**. Comanches hunted elk, black bears, and antelope but did not eat fish, birds, dog, or coyote. They captured or stole longhorn cattle. Large bison hunts had a leader, and each hunter knew his assignment. Hunters approached the bison and closed in. When they got within a few feet of the right side of the animal, the hunters sent an arrow down behind the last rib into the heart. Women did the rest of the work, including skinning the animals and removing the meat. Meat could be roasted or boiled, but the Comanche considered it bad luck to eat meat cooked both ways at the same meal.

Comanche men might wait to marry until after age 30. A man first had to have enough horses to support a wife. The groom took a gift, usually a horse, to the girl's parents or brother. If his proposal was accepted, the father or brother placed the horse among his own herd.

The Comanche had few rituals. There were no real leaders except a distinguished warrior chosen to lead during times of war. Within a band, a wise, older person was the peace chief. A council of **elders** helped decide when to move, whether to make war or peace, and the time of hunts. Gifted speakers spoke at treaty councils. Because each band was separate, a treaty with one band did not apply to the others.

In 1874 Quanah Parker led a large party to the Panhandle of Texas. The following year, the United States army surprised them in Tule Canyon and killed 1,000 horses. Without horses or food, Quanah Parker was forced to lead the Comanche to their **reservation**.

Comanche warriors used hard bison-hide shields. The rounded surface turned aside bullets and arrows. Warriors tied feathers to the rim to throw off the enemy's aim. Men decorated their shields with bear teeth while hunting, scalps while making war, and a horsetail while conducting raids.

Neighbors from the East

Tribes that came from the southeastern United States were generally peaceful farmers. Many southeastern tribes adopted the ways of white settlers in order to survive. The Cherokee, Seminole, Choctaw, Chickasaw, and Muscogee (Creek) became known as the "Five Civilized Tribes" of the United States.

Cherokee

Before the American Revolution (1775–1783), Cherokee land covered parts of North Carolina and surrounding states. After the Revolution, United States settlers and the U.S. government continued to push the Cherokee farther west off their lands. Some Cherokee eventually made their way into Texas. In 1819 Chief Bowles led 60 Cherokee families into Texas. They set up several villages north of Nacogdoches. On their farms along the Angelina, Neches, and Trinity Rivers they grew beans, squash, and corn.

The Cherokee readily adopted American **culture**, and some intermarried with whites. They still held onto some **traditions**, however. Cherokee society had seven **clans**, each associated with an animal. Marriage within a clan was forbidden. The Cherokee Green Corn Dance was a Thanksgiving celebration they held each year. They also played a game of stick ball similar to the modern game of lacrosse. A Cherokee named Sequoyah developed a written language for his people. Cherokee children were educated at American schools. Women wore American-style dresses. Men had a **turban** and a cloth coat tied at the waist with a sash. Some Cherokee had large farms that were worked by slaves, similar to the white population of the southeastern United States.

Sam Houston was an adopted Cherokee. He is shown here dressed as a Cherokee with the turban. Following Cherokee tradition, Houston never referred to himself as "I," but as "Houston."

The Cherokee asked Mexico for ownership of their land in Texas in the 1820s, but their claims were repeatedly denied or delayed. After Texas became independent, President Sam Houston arranged a treaty to grant them title to some of their land. But the Texas Senate never agreed to the treaty. The second president of the Republic of Texas, Mirabeau Lamar, ordered all tribes to leave Texas in 1839. The Cherokee, still without title to their land, decided to fight. In a battle near Tyler, Chief Bowles was killed. Many Cherokee fled to relatives in the Indian Territory in Oklahoma. Some went to Mexico. Others were **fugitives** in Texas. When Sam Houston returned as president of the Republic in 1841, he worked out a treaty with the Cherokee. However, the Cherokee never received payment for their land.

Wilma Mankiller

In 1985 Wilma Mankiller became the first woman to be chief of the Cherokee Nation. She earned the respect and attention of many with her efforts to improve communities and provide jobs and homes for American Indians. Mankiller left her job as chief in 1995, because of poor health. In 1998 President Bill Clinton awarded Mankiller the Presidential Medal of Freedom, the nation's highest **civilian** honor.

Choctaw

Choctaw legend says that the Choctaw and Chickasaw are **descendants** from two brothers. After moving west of the Mississippi River, the Chickasaw went north and the Choctaw went south. Over 700 Choctaw made their way into Texas in the 1830s.

A Good Start in Life

A newborn Choctaw child received gifts of a mare, colt, cow, calf, sow, and pigs. The animals could not be sold or given away. When the child was grown, he or she already owned a small herd.

The Choctaw tribe was divided into two groups. Besides the two large groups, the Choctaws were also divided into three districts. Each district had a *mingo*, or chief, elected by the men of the district. The three mingos met at a national council meeting to discuss issues concerning the tribe.

Choctaw marriage partners had to be from opposite groups, but young people were free to choose their mate. A young man made his affection known by throwing twigs at a girl. If she ran from the room, he was rejected. If she accepted, the groom brought presents to the bride's parents. On the day of the wedding, there was a feast. Then the bride and groom were led to separate houses. The bride was given a headstart to run to a pole on a distant hill. If the groom caught her before she reached the pole, her family showered her with gifts, and the couple were considered married. Children became members of the mother's group and were raised by their oldest uncle on their mother's side of the family. Adoption was common among the Choctaw.

The Choctaw in Texas built log cabins. **Cane** beds inside were raised off the floor and covered with deerskins. The beds also served as tables and chairs. The Choctaw raised corn, beans, melons, pumpkins, peas, sunflowers, and tobacco in their gardens. They kept herds of cattle that they sold to neighbors. Extra corn was stored for feed for the cattle. Choctaw women worked in the fields, made clothing, and prepared and stored food. Men hunted, built houses, made tools, governed the tribe, and protected the tribe during wars.

By 1830, the Choctaw had signed a treaty to move to Indian Territory in present-day Oklahoma. A few families were still in Nacogdoches and Shelby Counties at the time of the **Texas Revolution**. Choctaw dealings with the settlers were friendly. They boasted that they had never made war on whites. That did not save them from being moved out with other tribes in 1839. Some went to Mexico, while others went to Indian Territory.

Shawnee

A Missouri band of Shawnee arrived in Texas in 1822, and settled on the Red River. They were **allies** of the Cherokee and had friendly relations with white settlers. They even took part in the defeat of a Comanche force at Bandera Pass. Before they were moved to Indian Territory (Oklahoma) in 1839, the Shawnee negotiated payment for their crops and abandoned property. The Texas Shawnee went to Indian Territory as the Absentee Shawnee.

The Shawnee were on the move hunting during the winter. During summer months, they had large villages where they farmed corn, squash, and beans. The Shawnee built round, domed houses called wigwams. These were single-family homes made out of poles covered with bark. Shawnee men and women wore clothing made of animal skin, including leggings and moccasins. They often decorated their clothing with dyed porcupine **quills**, bright feathers, and paint. The Shawnee have been careful to pass down their **customs**. For that reason, they have better preserved their dances and religious **ceremonies** than other tribes.

This is a Shawnee participant in the yearly Red Earth Festival, which takes place in Oklahoma City, Oklahoma. The festival celebrates the American Indians of Oklahoma, which is where many tribes were forced to move in the 1800s.

Seminoles

The Seminoles did not permanently make their home in Texas, but they influenced it just by passing through. The Seminoles kept Africans called Seminole Blacks as slaves of the tribe. Most Seminole Blacks were runaway slaves who escaped from their American or British masters. The Seminoles allowed their slaves to live in separate communities. There they could work their own fields and have their own livestock. The Seminole slaves had to give some of their crop or livestock to their masters each year as their only requirement. The fact that the Seminoles allowed runaways to enter their community angered their white slaveholding neighbors. The Seminoles were pushed out of Florida in the early 1800s and made their way west.

This is a drawing of Chief John Horse, also known as Gopher John. He was a Seminole Black who led the group of Seminole slaves out of Texas and into Mexico from 1849 to 1850.

Each Seminole town had a *mico*, or head chief. There was also a group of less-important chiefs and a *heniha*. The *heniha* organized dances and **rituals** and made sure town buildings and fields were kept in good shape. The Seminoles farmed, and each family donated some of their crops to storage. Food kept in storage was used to help poor families and feed visitors. Besides farming, the Seminoles hunted, fished, and raised cattle. Seminoles wore a mixture of **traditional** and European clothing and jewelry. Seminole families lived in two buildings made with wooden frames. One building had two rooms. One room was used for sleeping and the other for cooking. The other building had two levels for storing potatoes, grain, and other food. It also had a covered balcony on the second floor, where guests were greeted and the family could find shade on hot days.

The Seminoles made their way into Indian Territory in the 1830s. The Creek Indians there tried to claim authority over the Seminoles and their slaves. Once Texas became part of the United States in 1846, the Seminoles decided to move to Mexico. Chief Wildcat (Coacoochee) and Seminole Black Chief John Horse led about 200 Seminoles and their slaves through Texas and into Mexico. The last part of their journey through Texas was a mad dash for the Rio Grande to avoid U.S. soldiers, who were coming to take the Seminole slaves. They made it across the river before the army arrived, and settled near Eagle Pass in Mexico.

After Chief Wildcat died in 1856, the Seminoles returned to Oklahoma because they had finally received their own land separate from the Creek. Wewoka, Oklahoma, is now the capital of the Seminole Nation of Oklahoma.

Seminole Blacks

Chief John Horse and the Seminole Blacks left Mexico in 1870. They moved to Fort Clark near Bracketville, Texas. Seminole Black scouts there helped the U.S. army in its actions against the Plains Indians of the area. A small cemetery near Bracketville contains the graves of four Seminole Black scouts who received the United States Congressional Medal of Honor for their service.

After years of service at Fort Clark, Seminole Blacks were still denied land in Oklahoma. Some of them stayed in Bracketville, and others returned to Mexico.

Texas Tribes Today

The three tribes in Texas today are the Tigua, Alabama-Coushatta, and Kickapoo. They are widely separated by distance, history, and **customs**.

Indian Reservations in Texas

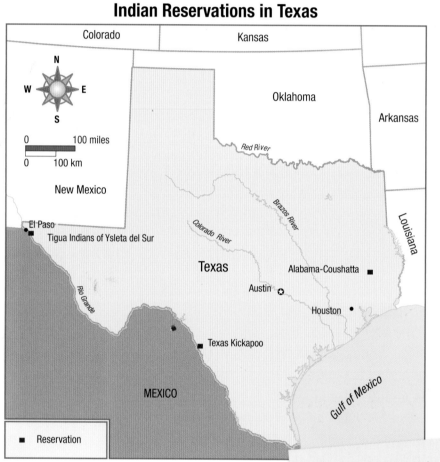

Of all the tribes that have lived in Texas, only three have **reservations** in the state today. Most tribes were forced to move to reservations in Indian Territory in the 1800s.

Tigua

In 1680 an uprising against the Spanish occurred in the **pueblos** along the upper Rio Grande. As a result of the Pueblo Revolt, Spanish priests and 317 Tigua (TEE-wah) Indians left Isleta Pueblo and traveled down the Rio Grande to El Paso. There they established Ysleta (is-LET-uh) del Sur, which means "little island of the south." The Tigua still claim Ysleta del Sur as their home, and the church there has operated continuously since that time.

Ysleta is really a **suburb** of El Paso. Modern houses sit on small lots, but some yards have a **traditional** beehive oven. Tigua from the Isleta Pueblo in New Mexico recognize the El Paso Tigua's claim to their **heritage**. However, many feel that the Tigua at Ysleta del Sur have become very Hispanic in their ways. Tigua tribal government has a religious leader who is elected for life by the tribal council. A governor is elected by the council to handle pueblo affairs. In modern times, some women have served on the tribal council.

The church at Ysleta del Sur was reconstructed for the third time in 1851, using what remained of the previous building. The silver bell tower was added in 1897.

The Tigua have been living in the region of Texas over 300 years. From Spanish times, authorities recognized their claim to the land at Ysleta. In 1967 Texas recognized the Tigua as a tribe. Today, a tribal center at Ysleta has shops that sell Tigua crafts, and dancers perform there. During celebrations, men wear colorful jackets trimmed in **calico** fringe. Women wear costumes adopted during the Spanish period.

Change in Country

The Rio Grande cut a new channel in 1830, making Ysleta del Sur an island. However, the Tigua were not in danger of being forced out by Texas President Lamar in 1839. Ysleta was still considered part of Mexico at the time. Ysleta del Sur became part of the United States under the terms of the 1848 Treaty of Guadalupe Hidalgo, which ended the Mexican War. Ysleta is now the oldest town in Texas.

The Tigua have used beehive-shaped ovens such as this for hundreds of years. They use the ovens to make tortillas and bread from the corn they grow.

Alabama-Coushatta

Alabama and Coushatta Indians lived along the Alabama River near Birmingham, Alabama, in the early 1700s. They shared a similar language and intermarried. When **game** became scarce, the two tribes went to Louisiana. They eventually drifted across the Sabine River into Texas. For some reason, Texas President Lamar did not make the Alabama and Coushatta leave when other tribes were removed from Texas in 1839.

By 1780, Alabama and Coushatta lived in the Big Thicket near Livingston. This unusual area is a thick tangle of growth with many kinds of wildlife. Trails made by the Alabama and Coushatta were the only way to get through the thicket. Alabama and Coushatta villages were a string of houses along a trail. Each house had a clearing for raising vegetables and fruit trees. Near the center of the line of houses, another clearing served as a place for **ceremonies**.

What's in a Name?

The word *Alabama* comes from words that mean "vegetation gatherers." The word *Coushatta* is another form of *Koasati*, which contains the word meaning "**cane**."

Both the Alabama and Coushatta tribes had a chief. In 1853, the Alabama chief asked the Texas **legislature** for a **reservation**. This was granted, and about 500 tribal members settled in Polk County, Texas. The Coushatta chief also asked for a reservation, but there was no suitable place near the Alabama tribe. The Alabama invited the Coushatta to share their land. After 70 years, the United States government enlarged the reservation and the Alabama-Coushatta Reservation became official. State funds were used to build houses, a hospital, and a gymnasium.

In 1939 the Alabama and Coushatta became a single tribe. They have a constitution with an elected seven-member council. The chief has an advisory position and votes only to break a tie. Alabama-Coushatta tribal land covers 2,800 acres (1,133 hectares). Of the 1,100 or so members, only about half live on the reservation. Many work in nearby communities. The **culture** center near Livingston features Alabama-Coushatta crafts and dances in traditional costumes. In Woodville, the Alabama-Coushatta conduct swamp buggy tours of the Big Thicket.

This Alabama-Coushatta boy from Texas was a powwow dancer at the yearly Red Earth Indian Festival in Oklahoma City, Oklahoma.

Kickapoo

After being pushed out of the Great Lakes area, the Kickapoo settled in Kansas. Trouble with white settlers split the tribe. Although some remained in Kansas, others came to Texas. Their attempt to settle with the Cherokee in Texas failed because of an argument over land. When American Indians were ordered out of Texas in 1839, some Kickapoo went to Indian Territory in present-day Oklahoma, and others went to Mexico. In 1850 some Oklahoma Kickapoo made the journey through Texas to Mexico with the Seminole. The Kickapoo also helped the Seminole fight the Plains Indians. When the Seminole returned to Oklahoma, Kickapoo took over their land at Nacimiento, Mexico, which is still their home.

Kickapoo medicine men are keepers of sacred bundles. These are animal-skin pouches containing sacred objects representing past glories of the tribe.

During the Civil War (1861–1865), some of the Oklahoma Kickapoo attempted to travel to Mexico. They were ambushed by Americans near San Angelo, but managed to fend off their attackers. They crossed the border into Mexico at Eagle Pass. For years they raided American border towns in revenge. Raids continued until Colonel Ranald Mackenzie's troops moved against the Lipan Apache and the Kickapoo. Some Kickapoo escaped, but others were captured and taken to Oklahoma.

The Mexican Kickapoo, as they call themselves, ignored the Rio Grande as an international boundary. They often built traditional **wickiups** and camped under the international bridge between Piedras Negras, Mexico, and Eagle Pass, Texas. In 1983 Mexico and the United States granted the Mexican Kickapoo dual citizenship. They are now free to cross the border when they wish.

The Kickapoo were not officially recognized in Texas until 1985. They were given land near El Indio and became the Kickapoo Traditional Tribe of Texas. There are also Kickapoo in Oklahoma and Kansas, but the keepers of the Kickapoo **traditions** live in Mexico. Part of the year, Mexican Kickapoo families are **migrant workers** in the United States, but they return to Nacimiento, Mexico. Their fierce hold on traditions preserves their culture and language.

Cynthia Leitich-Smith is a member of the Muscogee-Creek Nation and one of the 125,000 Texans with American Indian heritage. Cynthia lives in Austin, Texas, and writes books for children of all ages.

Life Today

Many place names in Texas are reminders of the tribes that have called the state home. Counties have names like Cherokee, Comanche, and Nacogdoches. There are towns named Comanche, Seminole, and East and West Tawakoni. There is also Caddo Lake and Kickapoo Creek.

More than names, though, the **descendants** of these tribes walk the streets of Texas towns and cities. They help shape the culture of the state with their rich traditions and history. Even though their people have been treated poorly in the past, Texas Indians have fought bravely in United States wars. They work many kinds of jobs and contribute to the welfare of Texas and the United States. Texas Indians also work hard to keep their heritage alive. Some participate in powwows and present demonstrations of traditional skills and crafts. Others search records and old documents to find links to tribes like the Karankawa and Coahuiltecan, which some thought had died out.

Too often, American Indians are portrayed as a vanishing people. However, statistics show that is not true. In 1900 there were only 470 American Indians living in Texas. One hundred years later, the **census** listed more than 125,000. These Texas American Indians are an important part of Texas's present and future.

Map of Texas

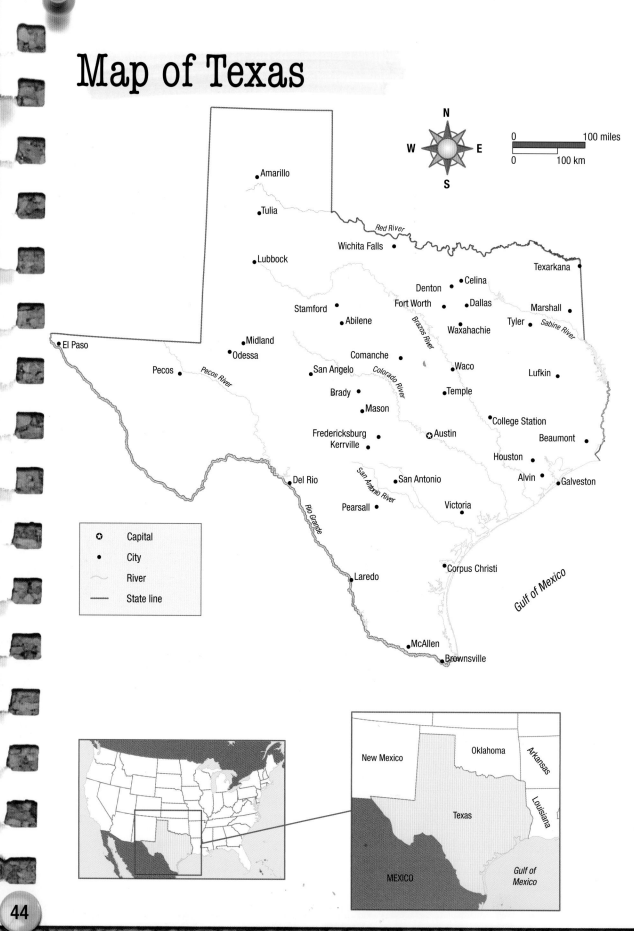

N
W   E
S

0   100 miles
0   100 km

Amarillo

Tulia

Red River

Wichita Falls

Texarkana

Lubbock

Celina
Denton
Fort Worth   Dallas
Marshall
Stamford   Waxahachie   Tyler   Sabine River
Abilene

Midland   Comanche
Odessa   Waco   Lufkin
Pecos   Pecos River   San Angelo   Colorado River
Brady   Temple
Mason
College Station
Fredericksburg   Austin   Beaumont
Kerrville
Houston
Del Rio   San Antonio River   San Antonio   Alvin   Galveston

Pearsall   Victoria

El Paso

Brazos River

Rio Grande

Laredo

Corpus Christi

Gulf of Mexico

✪   Capital
•   City
〰   River
—   State line

McAllen
Brownsville

New Mexico   Oklahoma   Arkansas

Texas   Louisiana

MEXICO   Gulf of Mexico

44

Timeline

9200–6000 BCE
Paleo-Indians live in Texas. They hunt ancient bison that are now **extinct**.

6000 BCE–700 CE
Plants and animals of today develop during the Archaic period. East Texas and Lower Pecos cultures gather food and hunt deer and bison. Artists create rock art along the Lower Pecos.

700–1600 CE
The Caddo develop a complex society and construct mounds in east Texas during the Late Prehistoric period.

1519
Hernando Cortés lands in Mexico. Alonso Alvarez de Pineda maps the Texas coast.

1528
Shipwrecked Cabeza de Vaca lands on Galveston Island.

1540
Spanish *conquistador* Coronado crosses the Panhandle looking for the Seven Cities of Gold. He probably meets the Apache there.

1682
The Tigua establish Ysleta Mission at El Paso.

1684
French explorer La Salle establishes Fort St. Louis on Garcitas Creek (Matagorda Bay).

1689
Spanish soldiers meet the Hasinai (Caddo) in east Texas and hear the word *Tejas*.

1719
San Antonio de Valero Mission (The Alamo) is built.

1750
The Comanche control the southern plains.

1800
The Tonkawa are in central Texas. The Wichita are along the Red River and near Waco. The Kiowa are in southwestern Oklahoma and the Panhandle.

1807
The Alabama-Coushatta and the Cherokee arrive in east Texas.

1820
Stephen Austin begins to bring white settlers into Texas.

1822
The Shawnee arrive in Texas.

1836
The Texas Revolution takes place and the Republic of Texas is formed.

1839
Texas president Lamar expels all tribes from Texas except the Alabama-Coushatta. Most tribes go to Oklahoma, but the Apache go to New Mexico.

1848
The Tigua are now in Texas after the Treaty of Guadalupe Hidalgo ends the Mexican War.

1850
Seminoles, Seminole Blacks, and Kickapoo cross through Texas on their way to Mexico.

1859
The final removal of Texas tribes to Oklahoma occurs.

1870
Seminole Blacks return to Texas.

1875
Quanah Parker and the Quahadi Comanche enter a **reservation** in Oklahoma.

1939
The Alabama-Coushatta incorporate as a single tribe.

1967
The Tigua are recognized as a tribe by the State of Texas.

1983
The Kickapoo are given land at El Indio and are recognized as the Texas Band of the Oklahoma Kickapoo.

2001
The 2000 U.S. **census** shows 420 people living on the Kickapoo Indian Reservation in Texas.

2004
The Smithsonian's National Museum of the American Indian opens in Washington, D.C.

Glossary

adobe brick made of earth or clay and dried in the sun

ally person or group of people who promise to help someone else

ancestor someone who came earlier in a family

artifact object made by humans, such as a tool, pottery, or a weapon

asphalt dark, sticky substance made from oil

breechcloth small piece of clothing worn around the hips

buckskin strong, soft leather made from the skin of a deer

calico cotton cloth with bright designs

cane often hollow, thin, and flexible plant stem

census official count of the number of people in a place

ceremony special act or acts done on special occasions

civilian person not on active duty in a fighting force

clan group of people who are related, usually by birth

climate weather conditions in an area

confederation group of peoples joined for some purpose

conquistador 16th-century Spanish soldier and leader, especially in the Americas

cradleboard small wooden frame on which an infant is strapped

culture way of life of a group of people, including their food, clothing, shelter, language, and practices

custom usual way of doing things

deity god

delicacy something good to eat that is unusual or difficult to find

descendant person who comes from a particular ancestor or family

drought period of time with little or no rain

elder person who has authority because of age and experience

excavate dig up and remove

extinct no longer living

fugitive person who has run away

game animal that is hunted for food

glacier large body of ice that moves slowly over a wide area of land

heritage something handed down from the past or from one's ancestors

Ice Age period of time when a large part of the earth was covered with glaciers and temperatures were lower

legislature governmental body that makes and changes laws

migrant worker laborer from another country or region who comes to work in the United States or a different region for a specific time

migrate move from one region to another, or pass from one region to another on a regular schedule

mission church community set up by traveling priests called missionaries

mollusk animal that usually lives in water and has an outside shell, such as an oyster

pueblo American Indian village of the southwest United States made up of groups of stone or adobe houses

quill one of the sharp, stiff spines that stick out on the body of a porcupine; also a large, stiff feather from the wing or tail of a bird

rawhide untanned animal skin

reservation land set aside by the government for American Indians

ritual established form for a ceremony or a system of rites

shaman religious leader of North American tribes, considered to have supernatural powers

sinew tough band of tissue that connects muscles with bones

smallpox very contagious and often deadly disease that causes a fever and sores on the skin

suburb city or town just outside a larger city

tallow white, solid fat obtained by heating the fatty tissues of an animal

tepee tent made of animal skins surrounding long poles and shaped like a cone

Texas Revolution war between Texas and Mexico that ended with Texas independence in 1836

thatch thick grass used as roofing

tradition belief or custom handed down from one generation to another

tributary stream flowing into a larger stream or a lake

tumpline headband woven to a basket to help carry the weight

turban head covering made of a long cloth wrapped around the head

turquoise greenish-blue semiprecious stone used in jewelry

wickiup shelter or hut with a round or oval base and a wood frame covered with reed mats or grass

Find Out More

Further Reading

Englar, Mary. *The Apache: Nomadic Hunters of the Southwest*. Mankato, MN: Capstone Press, 2003.

Roza, Greg. *The Karankawa of Texas*. New York: Rosen Publishing, 2005.

Sievert, Terri. *Texas*. Mankato, MN: Capstone Press, 2003.

Sonneborn, Liz. *The Choctaws*. Minneapolis, MN: Lerner, 2007.

Websites

http://www.native-languages.org/texas.htm
This site provides links to find out further information on the state's native peoples, as well as addresses for Texas's reservations.

http://www.texancultures.utsa.edu/nativeamerican/texas_native_americans/index.htm
The fascinating information on this site (from the University of Texas) is targeted directly towards fourth graders.

Index

Harris County Public Library
Houston, Texas